Emma Roberts

• • • •

Simply Fabulous!

• • • •

by Lauren Brown

Simon Spotlight

New York   London   Toronto   Sydney

SIMON SPOTLIGHT
An imprint of Simon & Schuster Children's Publishing Division
1230 Avenue of the Americas, New York, New York 10020
Text copyright © 2007 by Simon & Schuster, Inc.
All rights reserved, including the right of reproduction in whole
or in part in any form. SIMON SPOTLIGHT and colophon are
registered trademarks of Simon & Schuster, Inc.
Manufactured in the United States of America
First Edition
2 4 6 8 10 9 7 5 3 1
ISBN-13: 978-1-4169-0822-7
ISBN-10: 1-4169-0822-6
Library of Congress Catalog Card Number 2007920200

Dedicated to—

My Family:

Mom, Dad, Lindsie, Marc, Poppop, Aunt Shelly,
Uncle Michael, Madison, and Zachary

● ● ● ●

My Friends till the End:

You know who you are, and I love you all for
your never-ending support

● ● ● ●

My Light:

Grandma Mickey and Grandma Molly

Contents

Chapter 1

Just Having Fun

How do you stay a normal, all-American, everyday girl when you've spent your entire life smack dab in the middle of Hollywood? Just ask Emma Roberts! This five-foot-two, hazel-eyed cutie has her very own TV show, has starred in several major movies, and has had more than her fair share of face time with some of the biggest celebrities in the world. (In fact, she's even related to one of them.) Hanging out on movie sets is as normal for Emma as running around on a playground is for other kids. She's been a regular on soundstages and back lots since she was just a newborn baby! Emma has had an amazing opportunity to start her career early in life. Emma has enjoyed so much excitement in her life, it's hard to believe she's only sixteen!

Now no one would dare deny that the acting gene runs rampant in Emma Roberts's family! Her dad is Eric Roberts, from the hit ABC sitcom *Less Than Perfect*. Her aunt is the beloved actress Julia Roberts, who has an Academy Award displayed proudly on her mantel! And Emma's grandparents are renowned and established acting teachers. But her acting career isn't just about following in the footsteps of her famous and talented relatives and wanting to join the "family business." It's about making her lifelong dreams come alive. Emma's pursuing an acting career because she's following her heart.

Emma was a young child when she became confident that acting was her destiny. She often entertained her friends and family by re-enacting scenes from her favorite TV shows and movies. She was a pro at captivating any audience she could find with her dead-on impersonations and a variety of funny accents. So at nine years old, Emma effortlessly landed her first movie role in a big-budget film called *Blow*, which just happened to feature one of the biggest movie stars in the world. You might have heard of him—his name is Johnny Depp! Ever the ultimate professional, Emma wowed her famous costars with her confidence and commitment to making her performance in *Blow* one for the history books. They all agreed that she was wise beyond her years, and they knew she was on her way to becoming just as famous as her dad and aunt (maybe even *more* famous)!

Some people might assume that because Emma grew up in a family full of Hollywood heavyweights, she walks into her auditions with a chip on her shoulder. Or they might assume she doesn't even have to audition at all! Others might think nothing of the fact that her family is famous but assume that since Emma is young and successful she must have an inflated ego. After all, Hollywood has churned out plenty of horror stories about young stars who make ridiculous demands (like insisting on bowls full of green M&Ms in their dressing rooms, or expecting chauffeurs to drive them around town).

The stories can get even worse when it comes to Hollywood offspring-turned-actors. Many of them think they deserve leading roles without even auditioning and other crazy things like that just because they have a famous relative. But you will never catch Emma Roberts acting in such a disrespectful way. It makes no difference to her that she's been hanging around movie sets since she was two weeks old. It doesn't make Emma feel any more special than her other young Hollywood peers that her aunt Julia won an Oscar. Yes, Emma happened to grow up in a family full of Hollywood heavyweights, but she would never dream of pulling any kind of rank! When the *Birmingham Evening Mail* asked Emma what she thought of her famous aunt Julia, she simply responded, "If my career goes the same way as hers, that would be great!"

When you take away the part about being famous, Emma is just an average sixteen-year-old girl. And Emma's mom, Kelly Cunningham, makes sure fame will never change her daughter. If her mom ever notices even one tiny difference in Emma's attitude, the plug will be pulled on Emma's acting career on the spot. "We keep Emma grounded, teach her respect, not let her be spoiled and encourage her every day to appreciate what's been given to her," Kelly explained to the *New York Post*. Emma's fans look up to her because they can identify with Emma's offscreen life.

Emma recently left the Archer School for Girls in the Brentwood area of Los Angeles in favor of home schooling. Emma wasn't all that sad to leave her friends behind, as she has stayed just as close with them as ever. "My friends are so important to me. I'm lucky that I've had such close, strong, true friends ever since middle school," Emma told *Justine* magazine. "We keep our friendships strong by hanging out together every weekend. We go to the movies or the beach or shopping or just hanging out. When I need to hear a friendly voice, they're a cell phone call (or a Sidekick e-mail) away!"

Like every other teenager in America, she has homework and daily chores to do. Her chores can include anything from doing the laundry to cleaning her room or looking after her sister Grace. And she may be a big-time TV and movie star but even Emma isn't safe from getting grounded! "Sometimes I talk back to my mom and get in trouble," Emma told *ELLEgirl* magazine. "Don't all teenagers do that?"

In her spare time Emma loves keeping up with the latest fashion trends. Purses are her greatest weakness. She has an insanely huge collection that keeps growing! And if given the choice, Emma would much rather stay home to knit or cook than go out and party with the rest of young

Hollywood. As she told MSNBC, "I just hang out with my friends, family, play volleyball, and go to the movies—just normal kid stuff."

As the star of the hit Nickelodeon sitcom *Unfabulous*, Emma plays Addie Singer. Addie is an awkwardly adorable girl who anyone who has ever been in middle school can relate to. Addie's unique because she gets through the trials and tribulations of growing up by writing and singing songs about the humiliating and sometimes crazy events of her life. It's a role that Emma was born to play because Emma and Addie happen to have a lot in common. They both play the guitar and sing, and they both deal with friends, family, and figuring out how to get their crushes to confess their undying love for them. (Emma's crush happens to be on Adam Brody these days; Addie, on the other hand, loves a popular boy at school named Jake Behari.) Emma explained to *Entertainment Tonight* why so many girls relate to Addie's life on *Unfabulous*: "Like some girls, she wants to fit in. She wants to throw the best party, but at the same time she's happy with who she is," Emma said. "She's glad that she's getting through middle school and getting through life."

Emma loves spending her time on the *Unfabulous* set because the cast is filled with kids her own age. "I'm really having a lot of fun," Emma said on *Today*. "And it's great—it's a great set, a great show with great people, so I'm having a lot of fun with it." Emma's become really close friends with her cast mates—and they love her, too. Bianca Collins, who plays Addie's outrageous best friend Patti, gushed about their newfound friendship to *Popstar!* magazine. "Emma's so much fun!" she revealed. "We get along really, really well because we have the same type of personality. It's fun! She's so cute—I love her!"

The word on the street is that Emma will be seeing her name in lights for a long time to come. She earned rave reviews for her role in *Aquamarine* as a girl who discovers a mermaid in a swimming pool. Making the movie was one of the best times in Emma's life as she became close friends with her famous co-stars, Sara Paxton and JoJo. Emma's new big movie role is quite legendary, starring as the world's most famous teen sleuth, Nancy Drew, in *Nancy Drew*. "The really cool thing about the movie is that we're keeping Nancy Drew's character the same," Emma told *Teen* magazine. "She dresses in her cute, old-fashioned clothes and she is still sweet Nancy Drew."

Eloise DeJoria, Emma's costar in the movie *Grand Champion*, recently predicted in the *Chattanooga Times* that Emma's career will rival that of her famous aunt one day! "You'll see. Emma has that presence, like Julia [Roberts]. Everything that comes out of her mouth is right on target," Eloise explained. But even with the compliments (and a comparison or two to Julia), a hit TV show, and several movies under her belt, Emma stays grounded. She's just having a blast making her dreams come true. "I'm thrilled to be doing what I love, which is acting—but also being a normal kid,"

Emma explained to *Entertainment Tonight*. "I think it would be fun to be famous but I do it mostly because I enjoy acting and I think it's fun."

Emma's newfound fame has also given her another very important job that she takes quite seriously. With so many young girls watching *Unfabulous*, they look up to Emma and consider her a role model. And since Emma knows this is a big responsibility, she's quite careful to never do anything that might disappoint her fans. Emma's inspirations are her peers in the industry who haven't grown up too fast and have never let their fans down. Emma especially admires the careers of Mary-Kate and Ashley Olsen, and she gives singer/actress Hilary Duff big props. "I like that [Hilary] started off with a show on the Disney Channel and grew into this really popular actress doing good movies. I respect her," Emma told *USA Today*.

While so many other teen stars try to grow up too fast and hang out with a crowd twice their age or appear scantily clad on the cover of men's magazines, Emma plans on being her age for a long, long time to come. Emma really understands the responsibility she carries. As she told *Sweet 16*, "I know other girls my age are watching what I do, so I want to do it well."

Chapter 2

A Famous Family Tree

$\mathcal{E}$mma Rose Roberts was born on February 10, 1991, to Kelly Cunningham and Eric Roberts in Los Angeles, California. From the start it seemed almost inevitable that Emma would be an actress. After all, the acting gene was passed down from the Roberts side of the family tree. Emma's grandparents, Betty Lou Motes and Walter Roberts, were both renowned acting teachers in Atlanta, Georgia. Her grandfather founded the Atlanta Actors and Writers Workshop. Emma's dad, Eric, was already an established actor with a successful movie career when Emma was born. He had even been nominated for a Best Supporting Actor Oscar for the 1985 movie *Runaway Train.* Just like Emma, he started his acting career at a very young age. Eric was only seven years old when he started appearing on local TV shows in his hometown of Atlanta. Today you might remember Eric best as Will Butler, the vain yet lovable news anchor on the hit ABC comedy *Less Than Perfect.*

The acting bug didn't stop with Eric. It was also passed down to both his sisters, Emma's aunts, Julia and Lisa. Julia Roberts's very first acting job was costarring with her big brother in a little-seen film called *Blood Red.* She went on to become an Oscar-winning superstar. Lisa Roberts Gillan has been in movies such as *Raising Helen* and *Maid in Manhattan.* Lisa has had small roles in a lot of Julia's movies, including *Something to Talk About, Runaway Bride,* and *Mona Lisa Smile.* Acting is truly a family affair for the Roberts clan!

When Emma was just two weeks old, she got her first glimpse of the magical world of Hollywood. Hanging out on movie sets and back lots was just an ordinary day for this lucky baby, who often visited her dad on the set of his movie *Final Analysis*. It was definitely a taste of things to come in Emma's life—and probably the reason why Emma is not the least bit intimidated when she has to learn lines, take cues from directors, and rehearse on a set.

Despite the unusual experiences baby Emma was having in Hollywood, her home life wasn't quite picture-perfect. While Emma's parents loved her very much, they just weren't getting along with each other. When she was only six months old, her parents decided that it was best if they parted ways and got a divorce. Divorce is hard for children no matter how old they are, so it was surely a rough time for Emma even though she was just a baby. But Emma was fortunate. Relatives from both sides of her family were there to support her.

Even though her mom has full custody, Emma

still sees her dad all the time. And, in a way, the divorce of Emma's parents did have a bright side—it made Emma's family grow and grow. Today Emma lives with her mom; her stepdad, Kelly Nickels (the former bass player for the famous rock band L.A. Guns); and her half sister, Grace. Emma's dad is now married to Eliza, her stepmother, who is an actress and has been in several TV shows and movies, including the comedy classic *Animal House*. Eliza has two children, Morgan and Keaton, who are Emma's stepsiblings. She spends tons of time with her dad on the weekends and whenever they can find space in their busy schedules to see a movie or go to an amusement park. Emma and her dad are both regulars on the red carpet, and they've hung out at big Hollywood movie premieres together— like the one for Jim Carrey's film *Lemony Snicket's A Series of Unfortunate Events*.

Family is the heart and soul of Emma's life. She has a terrific relationship with both her parents and loves spending time with them. Her mom is very involved with Emma's career. There is rarely a time when she can't be with Emma, whether her daughter is on the set of *Unfabulous* or a movie. But there is another relative that Emma is extremely close to and looks up to greatly. Since Emma was a baby, she's practically been joined at the hip to her dad's little sister Julia.

When Emma was born, Julia Roberts was already one of the world's biggest movie stars. She had been nominated for an Oscar twice already—and her career was *just* picking up steam! In 1989 Julia had scored a nomination for her powerful portrayal of a new wife and mother who suffers from a fatal disease in the heartwarming movie *Steel Magnolias*. The next year, Julia was nominated again for her role in *Pretty Woman*. *Pretty Woman* was the movie that put Julia Roberts on the map! Even though she didn't win those Oscars, she did win Golden Globe Awards for both performances.

Julia's superstardom was something Emma hardly understood when she was a young girl. And even as Emma begins her own career today, Julia's fame has never affected their relationship. "When I'm with my aunt, we just cook or we'll hang out," Emma explained during an appearance on *Today*. "One time it was in the winter and we were at her house and I was on a little sleigh and we tied it to the back of the truck and she drove off and I was hanging on. That was a lot of fun." Sounds like a blast (and thankfully no one was hurt)!

And while Emma looks up to her famous aunt's career, she knows it's up to her—not her famous family surname—to keep her name in lights. "I think when people hear, 'Oh, that's Julia Roberts's niece,' they kind of obviously want to see if [I] can really act," Emma told *Justine* magazine. "So I think it's opened doors for me but hopefully it's me who got me where I am."

Emma and Julia Roberts not only have similar interests, they also look a lot alike. Aunt Julia is almost as famous for her acting as she is for her beautiful, megawatt smile. When people meet

Emma, one of the first things they notice is how much her smile and features remind them of Julia. Though if you ask Emma, she'll most likely disagree. "I think we both have the same smile," Emma told *USA Today*. "But I don't think I look like her at all." One of the first things Ellen DeGeneres said when Emma appeared on her talk show was that she looked just like Julia. "Yes, that's what I'm told," Emma responded. Even when Ellen held up a poster of Emma and Julia to do a side-by-side comparison, Emma still wasn't convinced, even with the audience oohing and aahing in agreement! One thing is for sure, though: Both Emma and her aunt are equally beautiful in their own right!

Maybe people think that Emma looks like her aunt Julia because they spend so much time hanging out together! When Julia's busy schedule of making movies started to make it harder for her to see her friends and family (especially Emma), she came up with a great idea. She started inviting Emma to visit her on the sets of some of the movies she was making. They would miss each other way too much otherwise!

Hanging around Julia's movie sets always guaranteed that Emma was going to walk away with some incredible memories. Especially since Julia always had some amazing costars! "I remember one time when Aunt Julia was making [the movie] *Conspiracy Theory*," Emma told the *New York Post*. "I said, 'Hey, Mom, meet my friend Mel [Gibson]!' Everyone was looking at me like I was crazy."

In 2000 Emma visited Julia on the Las Vegas set of the romantic comedy *America's Sweethearts*. Julia's costars were some of the biggest movie stars around—Catherine Zeta-Jones, John Cusack, and Billy Crystal, just to name a few!

"Catherine Zeta-Jones was so cool. At the wrap party for *America's Sweethearts* there was karaoke and I sang a song," Emma recalled to *Teen* magazine. "So, Catherine signed her autograph to me, 'Emma, it was really great to hear you sing tonight. Love, Catherine Zeta-Jones.' So that was really cool!"

Emma was in awe as she spent time on the set. But the best part was a special surprise Julia arranged for her. Emma actually got to be in the movie as an extra! There's no denying that sometimes who you know does help!

In 1999 Emma was invited to visit Julia on the set of a drama called *Erin Brockovich*. The movie was based on the true story of a single mother who worked as a legal assistant and almost single-handedly brought down a California power company accused of polluting a city's water supply. While Emma wasn't cast as an extra in this film, she had an even more meaningful experience on the set. Emma watched her aunt film scenes that would eventually win her the Best Actress Oscar. You couldn't ask for a better acting lesson than that!

And on the special night that Julia Roberts accepted her prestigious award in front of millions of viewers from around the globe, she thanked Emma in her acceptance speech! Can you imagine how Emma must have felt? All of Julia's fans around the world now knew what a special part Emma played in her life! The entire experience has stuck with Emma ever since. She even told the New York *Daily News* that she wanted to win an Oscar one day too . . . just like her aunt Julia!

Johnny Depp and Other Adventures in the Movies

With an Oscar winner in the family, it was inevitable that Emma was going to turn out to be an amazing actress herself! No one in her family was surprised when Emma announced at the age of nine that she was ready to pursue an acting career of her own. In fact, they had just been waiting for the day Emma would say it out loud. Emma's mom, however, was a little worried about Emma trying her hand at acting at such a young age. Kelly wasn't in show business (and never has been), but she knew Emma was facing a tough road ahead that could be filled with disappointments. She wasn't being pessimistic, and it wasn't that she didn't foresee big things for Emma. She was just looking out for her daughter. She didn't want Emma to be disappointed if she got rejected for a part she really wanted. Kelly also worried that acting might prevent Emma from having a normal childhood. But she decided that if Emma really and truly wanted to act, she wouldn't stop her. But there were a few conditions that Emma had to comply with: She had to continue going to school, playing with her friends, and doing her chores. Essentially, she had to stay "normal."

"[Acting] is what Emma wants, so I'm into it one hundred percent. But that's with the understanding that she must go to college," Kelly told the *New York Post*. "Life is a long road and she's got to be prepared for it." Emma agreed but she did complain to the *New York Post* once that her mom constantly reminded her to "keep up her grades" or she wouldn't be able to continue acting. Despite her mom's concerns, acting was Emma's passion, so she was fully prepared to make the commitment and stick with it. "I always remember wanting to be an actress ever since I was little," Emma told Al Roker during an appearance on *Today*. "I would go around the house with an English accent or saying lines from a TV show. So I just always remember wanting to do this. I really asked my mom, 'Mom, can I act? Can I go on auditions?' and I don't think she wanted me to get into it too early," Emma explained.

Emma's aunt and dad were proud and delighted to welcome a new actor into the family. As Emma began going to auditions, they gave her advice, support, and encouragement. "My dad and aunt are so excited for me," Emma told *Popstar!* magazine. "They just said 'Congratulations, be yourself, and have a great time.'" But Eric and Julia agreed with Kelly; they also wanted Emma to have a normal life. "My dad is very proud I've made the decision to act," Emma told the *New York Daily News*. And even though Emma and Julia rarely talked shop, Emma didn't keep it a secret that she wanted an acting career that was just as successful as Julia's! "She's inspired me a lot. She's my role model. Aunt Julia thinks my [acting] is great, but she also thinks I should be a kid outside playing and things like that. I think she's great at acting. I want to grow up to be just like her," Emma told the British paper *The Sunday Mail*.

When Kelly let Emma go on her first audition, for a movie called *Blow*, no one dared to believe that she would get the part! After all, it was her first audition. But Emma beat the odds—and then some!

Blow was based on the true story of George Jung, the man responsible for bringing cocaine to the United States in the seventies. Johnny Depp had already been cast as George, and Emma was auditioning for the role of Kristina Jung, his daughter. Johnny is one of the most talented actors in Hollywood—and it doesn't hurt that is he also one of the most handsome! He's played a diverse and complex range of characters in movies such as *Pirates of the Caribbean, Charlie and the Chocolate Factory, and Finding Neverland*. "I was so young. I didn't understand that I was working with one of the best actors ever until later," Emma told *ELLEgirl*. The cast was filled with other amazing stars too, like acclaimed actress Penélope Cruz, who played Kristina's mother. Penélope was well known in the United States as well as in her native country, Spain, starring in films such as *All the Pretty Horses* and *Vanilla Sky*. Ted Demme, who was a well-respected director in Hollywood, had signed on to direct *Blow*.

When Emma was offered the part of Kristina, her first reaction was complete shock! "My mom was like, 'You know, we'll send her on the audition [for *Blow*], it'll keep her quiet for a while, you know, it's her first audition . . . she probably won't get the part,'" Emma said on *Today*. "And so we went on it and then we got a callback and me and my mom were like 'Wow!'"

Kelly admitted to *People* magazine, "I thought it would pacify her . . . and then she got the job." Emma had a lot of competition from other young actresses for the role of Kristina—many who had a lot more experience than Emma! "I was up against a lot of girls," Emma told the *Vancouver Sun*. "I was amazed [when I got the part]. I was like 'What? What?'"

When the initial shock of landing the part of Kristina wore off, Emma admitted that the experience was a little overwhelming. "I was nervous because it was my first audition, but I was pretty prepared. I have an acting coach; I don't really ask my aunt Julia for advice," Emma told the *New York Daily News*. And even though Emma was playing someone close to her own age, the role of Kristina was incredibly demanding. For starters, part of the movie took place in the 1980s. So Emma's wardrobe was filled with clothes from a decade before she was even born! "I wore these hideous outfits 'cause it was the eighties," Emma told *People* magazine. "I'd wear little dresses that poof out, and my hair would be on the side of my head, all curly. How could people dress like that?"

Style wasn't the only difference with Kristina that Emma had to overcome. Kristina's life was very different from Emma's, so Emma had to find a dark place deep inside in order to convincingly portray the daughter of a man who pushed drugs and ran from the law. "I had to act depressed and mad," Emma told the *New York Daily News*. "It wasn't too hard. I just didn't smile, and I tried not to be funny." Spoken like a true pro!

Eric was proud that Emma's first acting job was in such a big and important movie. "I am enormously proud of my daughter," he bragged to the British newspaper *The Mail on Sunday*. "She always reads her own scripts. I asked her why she chose this one, thinking she would tell me it was because she liked Johnny Depp. And she looked at me and said, 'Daddy, I get to say the *F* word four times.' It was hysterical." Frequent use of the *F* word was probably the least graphic and disturbing aspect of the movie. *Blow* received an R rating because it featured scenes with drug use and was really graphic.

Emma's parents decided that she could act in the movie but she couldn't see it until she was older! Everyone on set, especially director Ted Demme, "made sure I wasn't around the bad stuff," Emma told *USA Today*. Till this day, Emma has yet to see *Blow* in its entirety. "I just got a tape with all my parts [in the movie]. But I can see any PG-13 movie I want," Emma told *People* magazine. Emma didn't quite plan on having her movie debut in an R-rated film. "It just came up," she explained to the *Daily News*. "Now I'd go for more family comedies." Emma's mom told *USA Today* that Emma will be allowed to watch *Blow* from start to finish when she is eighteen years old. Emma, however, is trying to change that rule to when she is sixteen or seventeen years old.

The entire cast and crew of *Blow* truly adored working with Emma. By the time filming wrapped, they all predicted that big things were ahead for her. Ted Demme told *People* magazine, "Emma was never intimidated by tough scenes. I see an enormous future for her." But most impressive of all was that the film critics loved Emma's performance. Often their harsh write-ups can make or break careers, and they were all extremely impressed with Emma's acting debut. When the reviews came out, critics unanimously thought Emma gave a breakthrough performance. The *Palm Beach Post* in Florida even called her a "scene stealer." With just one movie on her resume, Emma was already an enormous success!

Chapter 4

A Star on the Rise

In Hollywood it takes just one standout performance to put an actor in high demand. But what if that standout performance is opposite big-time stars? If your performance steals even a little bit of their thunder, then by Hollywood standards, you've got it made! That's why Emma's heartfelt and memorable performance in *Blow* had double the impact. After all, her costars were big-time celebrities like Johnny Depp and Penélope Cruz— and Emma still stole the show! Everyone in her family was bursting with pride. Emma's mom gave all the credit to the Roberts side of the family for Emma's success. "I think genetics play into it. She's not afraid of being in front of people, which I'm terrified of doing," Kelly told the New York *Daily News*. "She definitely got that from the Roberts side . . . and she's got the Julia Roberts smile." Emma's dad couldn't stop bragging about the Roberts family's newest star to anyone and everyone who would listen. "There would be no one happier than me if my daughter was to become a huge success," he told *The Mail on Sunday*. "Emma Roberts could be the next big star. She could be the next Julia. It could happen."

With so much support and encouragement from her family, Emma was hooked on making movies and wanted to keep the momentum of her career going full steam ahead. Next for Emma was a short independent film called *BigLove*. It was a quirky fantasy about two neurotic parents who don't want their children to go to school, so they do outlandish things to try and stop them. Emma played one of the kids named Delilah. Sam Rockwell (you might know him from the first *Charlie's Angels* movie) and Mary McCormack (she's been in movies like *K-Pax*) played her parents. *BigLove* made its world premiere at the Sundance Film Festival, which is a prestigious event founded by renowned actor Robert Redford to celebrate the best in independent films for the coming year. Huge stars usually attend the event, whether or not they have a movie opening there, because it's an extravaganza that's not to be missed. The ten-day-long festival is filled with fabulous parties, elegant dinners, and lots of skiing! However, Emma had to sit out *BigLove*'s Sundance debut—her mom gave birth to her sister, Grace, the week of the festival. Emma was a little disappointed, but she also really wanted to be home to greet the newest member of her family!

After Emma made *BigLove* (which garnered rave reviews at Sundance), she didn't have to look very hard for another opportunity to act. In fact, her next role literally came looking for her! Julia Roberts was good friends with an actor by the name of Barry Tubb. He had appeared in movies such as *Top Gun* and *Mask*, but he really wanted to try his hand at directing. Because of Barry's friendship with Julia, he had known Emma since she was a little girl and had always been intrigued and amused by Emma's engaging personality. "I was writing [a different] movie when Emma was six years old. She came in and was saying the funniest things ever," Barry recalled to the *San Antonio Express-News*. "I said to her aunt Julia, 'I'm going to write a movie for Emma. What do you think?' Julia goes, 'Ask Emma.'" Fast forward to a few years later when Barry used Emma as his muse for a family adventure movie he was writing called *Grand Champion*. "I wrote it for Emma," Barry told the *Dallas Morning News*. And since the movie was written just for Emma, she got to star in it!

Grand Champion is the story of a poor family who was forced to sell their beloved calf (named

Hokey Pokey) in order to make ends meet. Emma was the younger sister of Buddy, played by newcomer Jacob Fisher, who leads his friends on a mission to kidnap Hokey Pokey after they learn that his new owner plans on turning him into barbeque meat. Joey Lauren Adams, who had starred in *Chasing Amy* and *Big Daddy*, played Emma's mom.

Emma was really proud of *Grand Champion* and loved every minute she spent on the set. "My character doesn't even have a name. I'm just 'the sister,' which was funny," Emma told the *Fort Lauderdale Sun-Sentinel*. "I'm really Buddy's sidekick in the adventure. Jacob was very nice to work with. Joey plays our mother, who gets mad when I tell her what's going on. It was so much fun to do, especially as I got to go to Texas, where I'd never been before and I loved it there. We shot for six weeks in Snyder, Texas, and I got to hang out with a lot of other kids, and we all learned so much about cattle and that whole way of life. I mean, I grew up in L.A., so it was a real education." Emma also really liked working with the steer that played Hokey Pokey.

"In real life Hokey Pokey's actually two steers. One is for stunts and one is for regular stuff," she told the *Arizona Daily Star*. "They needed Pokey to gallop like a horse in one scene but the regular Pokey was kind of lazy and wouldn't do it. So that's when they brought in the stunt steer who was like the top steer around!"

Since the movie was filmed in rural Snyder, Texas, it was not the most glamorous of movie sets. Besides the rustic location, the entire movie was also made on a very limited budget. But what the set lacked in glamour, it made up for in fun! "We spent what Hollywood spends on their potato chips and soda pops. We didn't have a lot of money, but we had a lot of friends. No one did this for money. Hopefully they liked the story and they wanted to see it do something," Barry told the *San Antonio Express-News*. "I think the world's ready for a good heartwarming story. You don't have to cover your

kids' eyes and cover their ears when they watch it."
Plus, Julia Roberts was a regular visitor on the set!
She came down to support her friend Barry, and
of course spend time with Emma. So since Julia
was there so much, she ended up with a small part
in the movie. Imagine how great it was for Emma
to act side by side with her aunt! "My aunt plays
this pregnant lady, Jolene. We're pretty close, so
we were able to hang out on the set together and I
stayed with her for a couple of weeks," Emma told
the *Fort Lauderdale Sun-Sentinel*. "People always
ask me if she gives me lots of advice, but we really
don't talk about movies or the business. We'll cook
or talk about fashion, that kind of thing."

Julia wasn't the only star hanging around the set
of *Grand Champion*. Bruce Willis, Natalie Maines
from the Dixie Chicks, and country singer George
Strait all had cameos in the movie too! Having
Bruce Willis on set was a big treat for Emma. Her
good friend is his daughter, Scout, though Emma
denied that she had anything to do with her friend's

dad getting a part in the movie! "I think Bruce knew other people, including my aunt, and just really wanted to be in it and he was great fun to be around," Emma told the *Fort Lauderdale Sun-Sentinel*. "He'll sit and talk with kids just the same as if he's with adults, which is cool." And having her aunt on the set wasn't just comforting and familiar for Emma. Having Julia around kept Emma's costar, Natalie Maines, calm. *Grand Champion* was her first movie role, and Natalie told the *San Antonio Express-News* that Julia helped her through it. "She was like my wardrobe girl and my stage mom. Thank God she was there or I'd never have made it," Natalie said.

When they finished filming the final scene of the movie, George Strait paid homage to the beloved Hokey Pokey by actually singing the "Hokey Pokey" song (you know how it goes: "You put your right foot in, you put your right foot out!") for the entire crowd of two thousand people who were watching. "That's why I hope all different ages will like the film," Emma told the *Arizona Daily Star*. "It's got kids like us and the steer, and it's also got people like my aunt and Bruce Willis. I think it's pretty unusual."

Working on *Grand Champion* gave Emma new experiences—from the chance to explore a new city to the opportunity to act with her aunt. But there was one other very special thing that starring in *Grand Champion* brought to Emma's life: a new uncle! A cinematographer by the name of Danny Moder was working as a cameraman on *Grand Champion*. Danny and Julia were already good friends because they had worked together on the movie *The Mexican*. When Julia and Danny reunited on the set of *Grand Champion*, it became evident that they were more than just old friends— they were in love! On July 4, 2002, not long before filming on *Grand Champion* wrapped, Julia married Danny Moder in a private ceremony at her ranch in New Mexico. If it wasn't for Emma and her acting career, it's quite possible that Aunt Julia and Uncle

Danny might never have crossed paths again and been reunited! And that story gets even better: On November 28, 2004, Julia gave birth to twins: a girl named Hazel Patricia and a boy named Phinnaeus Walter! "She had been wanting to start a family for a while and I am thrilled it has finally happened!" Emma told London's *Evening Star*.

Emma and Julia are so close that Julia made sure that Emma was one of the first to know she was expecting. "The day before it was in every single magazine, Aunt Julia called me and told me [she was pregnant]," Emma told *Entertainment Tonight*. "And I thought that was really great." When the babies were born, Emma was psyched that she had new cousins to brag about to the world. "I'm so excited," Emma told *People* magazine about the babies. "I'm going to spoil them. I'll be the babysitter whenever [Aunt Julia] needs!" Even though Emma has a younger sister to play with, she was very much looking forward to having new little babies to hold in her arms because, as she told *Entertainment*

Tonight, "[My baby sister] was born so big!" And like any true fashionista, as soon as the babies were born, Emma started putting aside some money from her weekly allowance of twenty dollars to buy them clothes. "I already have some outfits in mind," she told *People* magazine. Unfortunately Emma's crazy work schedule has made it harder for her to hang out with her little cousins as they get older. "I don't have time to baby-sit the twins that much! But I hang out with Aunt Julia and Hazel and Phinnaeus when I can," Emma told *Teen* magazine. And ever the proud cousin, Emma can't stop bragging about how adorable they are. "Hazel is so cute—she looks like Dakota Fanning in baby form—she has these big blue eyes. And Phinnaeus is adorable too." Who knows? Maybe one day Hazel and Phinnaeus will decide to follow their famous cousin's footsteps and have their *own* acting careers!

Chapter 5

Simply Fabulous!

After the blast Emma had making *Grand Champion*, it didn't seem like anything could top that experience. After all, the movie was written just for her! And who could forget that it was the setting where Julia fell in love with her husband, Danny! But soon after *Grand Champion* finished filming, Emma was cast in another movie that seemed like it was going to be thrilling too. She was right! The movie was called *Spymate* and one of Emma's costars was a chimpanzee! As an animal lover, Emma couldn't have been more excited. In *Spymate*, she played a twelve-year-old inventor named Amelia who wins a big prize for inventing the prototype of a revolutionary chemical drill. But she ends up getting kidnapped by an evil doctor who wants to make a bigger version of Amelia's drill and take over the world.

Playing a science genius was fun because, as Emma told the *Vancouver Sun*, "It's something I'm not!" But the best part about making the movie was filming scenes with her primate costar. "He's cute," Emma told *People* magazine about the chimpanzee. "But you can't distract him or he'll start kissing and hugging you when he's not supposed to." Emma got a kick out of the experience. "I was really excited that there was a chimp," she said in her *Sun* interview. "They're really sweet, and it's incredible to see that they're animals and they're working like that." Emma's friends were extremely jealous that not only did she get to make a movie but that she also got to hang out with a chimp all day! "One of my friends said, 'You know, I could come to the set with you anytime.' And I'm like, 'Yeah, you can,' and she's like, 'Yeah, like maybe one of those days when the chimps are there?'" Emma told the *Vancouver Sun*. Emma had to be tutored on the set of *Spymate* since it was being filmed in the Canadian city of Vancouver, and her school was in L.A. But even though Emma missed seeing her friends every day, she handled being away from them in a mature way. "I'm a very social person, so it's not like a big loss for me because I still talk to my friends and all," she told the *Vancouver Sun*. Emma also had lots of great costars to keep her entertained. Richard Kind, the funny man from the sitcoms *Spin City* and *Scrubs*, played the evil scientist, and Debra Jo Rupp from *That 70s Show* starred in *Spymate* too.

After *Spymate* wrapped, Hollywood was abuzz with the news that Emma was poised to become a very big star. The children's cable TV channel Nickelodeon was especially impressed with Emma's budding career and asked her to meet with them about projects they had in the works. This was a huge opportunity for Emma! After all, Nickelodeon was famous for launching the careers of some of the biggest names in young Hollywood. Amanda Bynes went from Nickelodeon shows such as *All That* and *The Amanda Show* to big movies such as *What a Girl Wants* and her own TV show on The WB called *What I Like About You*. Nick Cannon appeared on the popular show *All That* and went on to star in movies such as *Drumline* and *Love Don't Cost a Thing*. And perhaps most impressive is Kenan Thompson's career path. He starred on the Nickelodeon show *Kenan & Kel* before moving on to a regular spot on *Saturday Night Live*. He recently played the title role in the live-action movie version of the classic cartoon *Fat Albert*.

Emma knew that a TV show with Nickelodeon could take her career to the next level. The pressure of this meeting may have been too much for other kids to take, but Emma stayed calm—and she was a big hit with Nickelodeon executives! "We had a great meeting and came away very impressed by her," Nickelodeon's senior vice president of talent, Paula Kaplan, raved to the *Hollywood Reporter*.

So when Nickelodeon had a new sitcom in development called *Unfabulous*, they knew that Emma would be perfect for the lead role of Addie Singer. Before long, Emma was starring in her very own show! *Unfabulous* is about a girl in seventh grade named Addie who deals with everything kids her age face on a daily basis: fitting in at school, getting noticed by her crush, and getting along with her family. What makes Addie special is that she writes songs about everything going on in her life and sings them too! You could say that Addie's songs are like writing in a journal. Emma described Addie to *Popstar!* magazine as being "very creative." Addie "goes through what most teens go through—angst with family, friends, boys, and school. She expresses herself through music and songwriting." Emma and Addie are a lot alike. "We both play guitar! We're both curious and like to try new things and just take things day by day," Emma told *Popstar!*. "But I'm a little more outgoing than Addie. I say my opinion more!"

Getting the chance to sing and play the guitar in each episode was an added bonus for Emma. She loves to sing and has taken guitar lessons since she was nine years old. "I always took guitar lessons and complained, 'Mom, I'm not going to guitar lessons,'" Emma told *Entertainment Tonight*. "She said, 'It'll pay off,' and when it did, I was like, 'Okay, you're right!'"

Learning Addie's songs is fun for Emma because they're usually silly little numbers that are easy to play and memorize. All of the songs—including the show's theme song—are written by singer/songwriter Jill Sobule. Even though Jill writes all the words and music, Emma really sings and plays the guitar in every episode. But if Addie sometimes sounds a little off-key, don't hold that against Emma. "Addie's actually really good at playing the guitar, but singing? She's not supposed to be the best," Emma explained to U.dailybulletin.com. "I relate to her like Phoebe from *Friends* . . . only a little bit better." Emma loves that she gets to sing all the time on the show. "I've never been trained in singing," she explained to *People* magazine. "But ever since I was little I would sing in front of the camera all the time!" Emma's rock-and-roll fantasies first came true in the spring of 2005 when she recorded the song "If I Had It My Way" for the Disney movie *Ice Princess*. And Emma did such an amazing job singing on *Unfabulous* that in the fall of 2005, she released a soundtrack to the show called *Unfabulous and More: Emma Roberts*, where she sang all ten songs on the album. Six of the songs are from the first season of the show, including classic tunes such as "Punch Rocker" and "New Shoes." The other four songs are brand-new, including a song called "This Is Me," which Emma helped write! "The songs are really fun and playful—and yes, they do kind of describe me. I wanted to pick songs that I could relate or that

I thought other people could relate to," Emma said in the CD's press release. "My favorite song to record was 'I Wanna Be.' I can really relate to it because it's more than just a story. It's saying that I want to have fun and I want my life to mean something." Right now, Emma is planning on giving music a break while she focuses on her acting career—but never say never when it comes to the prospect of Emma singing again!

Emma found out she got the part of Addie from her mom, who decided not to reveal the big news right away. "I came home from school and asked my mom if she had heard anything and she said 'No,'" Emma told *Popstar!* magazine. "That night, she took me out with my family and said, 'Congratulations! You got the part!'" Emma was ecstatic that she was only twelve years old and had her very own TV show! Nickelodeon was proud to have Emma on board. They knew Emma was going to be the next big thing. "Emma Roberts brings [Addie Singer] to life with just the right balance of comedy, quirkiness and heart as Addie journeys down the bumpy road of adolescence," Cyma Zarghami, the president of Nickelodeon, declared in a press release sent out to the members of the Television Critics Association. Sue Rose, the creator and executive producer of *Unfabulous*, said, "Working with Emma is the icing on the cake. She's extremely talented, a doll, and a joy to work with. Her honesty and charm add a dimension to the character and bring a realness to the show." You couldn't ask for bigger compliments than that!

Emma is also extremely lucky to have an amazing cast of costars on the set of *Unfabulous*. They all became one big happy family pretty much from day one. "The first day of filming *Unfabulous* was so much fun. I actually didn't mind getting up at six a.m. because I was so excited to meet and work with everyone," Emma wrote on the blog she keeps on the nick.com website. "Seeing my wardrobe, set and costars was a lot of fun. Going to the set is like my home away from home." Most of the kids starring on *Unfabulous* with Emma had very little—if any—acting experience. Compared to them, Emma was an old pro, so she was more than happy to help them calm their nerves and make them feel comfortable. "I've been around TV sets all my life because of my dad," she told *Tiger Beat*. "So this feels totally normal to me."

One of Emma's favorite parts of filming *Unfabulous* is rummaging through her wardrobe closet! It is stocked with the most adorable clothes, shoes, and accessories that she gets to wear. And there is another perk that Emma loves—she gets her hair and makeup done every morning before filming begins! "I'm young so my makeup is very simple," Emma told *Tiger Beat* magazine. It takes just thirty minutes for the hair stylists and makeup artists to get her camera-ready!

Emma was having so much fun filming episodes of *Unfabulous* and hanging out with her cast mates that she forgot one very important thing: The show was going to air on TV! Emma really loved the show and the plot lines, and she knew the rest of the cast did too. But they had no idea if the rest of the world would love it until it finally aired. *Unfabulous* was to air on Sunday nights at 7:30 p.m. during the block of programming dubbed TEENick. *Drake & Josh*, *Ned's Declassified School Survival Guide*, and *Romeo* were the other shows on that night too. During commercial breaks, various celebrities ranging from Lindsay Lohan to TEENick stars hosted minisegments with music, games, and comedy. With *Unfabulous* surrounded by popular shows and fun segments, deep down, everyone knew that it couldn't miss!

The first episode of *Unfabulous* made its debut on September 12, 2004. Emma was a nervous wreck! "I was scared and excited at the same time. I didn't think I would be nervous but when the time came I was actually really nervous," Emma wrote on nick.com. "I didn't have a big party. I just watched it with my family and manager." It was really weird for Emma to see herself playing Addie on TV. She couldn't believe that other kids all over the country were watching her at the exact same time she was watching with her family!

"When I watched the show, I really liked it, even though it was weird wondering if any of the other kids my age would be watching it and *not* like it!" Emma added on the nick.com website. "After the show, I was relieved and really happy because all my family and friends called me to tell me what a good job I did. I was so happy for all my fellow cast members and everyone who worked on the show."

Unfabulous was off to an incredible start. The ratings were high and the critics loved it. They all agreed on one very important thing—Emma rocked! When *Variety* reviewed the show, they said that Emma's "comic delivery, sly smile, and diminutive stature for her age make her much more relatable . . . to tween girls."

A reviewer for the *St. Louis Post Dispatch* raved, "At thirteen, Emma Roberts potentially has decades in front of the camera yet to come." With so much positive feedback, Emma and the rest of her cast mates could relax and just have a blast making the show!

A Home Away from Home

Sure, Emma is the star of *Unfabulous*, but each of her cast mates adds something special and unique to the show. We already know how much family means to Emma, so let's take a few minutes to meet Emma's extended family—the talented cast of *Unfabulous*.

Molly Hagan. Molly plays Addie's sarcastic mom, Sue. She's a "cool" mom who Addie can relate to because they're more like two friends than mother and daughter. Molly's been in a ton of big movies and TV shows so you might recognize her from a guest stint on *Friends* (she played the teacher in a cooking class that Monica and Joey took) or the dark comedy *Election*, which stars Emma's favorite actress, Reese Witherspoon!

Markus Flanagan. Markus plays Addie's dad, Jeff. He's the manager of a sporting goods store and just can't understand why his little girl has to grow up and start liking boys! You might have seen Markus in guest appearances on some popular TV shows such as *Will & Grace* and *Friends*.

Tadhg Kelly. Tadhg plays Addie's hot older brother, Ben, who's very well liked at his high school. He's also the object of affection for most of the girls at Addie's middle school—especially the popular ones! In real life Tadhg is eighteen years old and toured with musicals and choir groups before getting his big break on *Unfabulous*. "This is the best job I could have ever hoped for," he told *Tiger Beat*. Tadhg and Emma really hit it off because they have a lot in common, including making music. "I can sit and write a song for hours," Tadhg told *Tiger Beat*.

Even though Tadhg and Emma give each other a hard time as brother and sister on the show, they really love and respect each other in real life. "Emma is always full of energy. She's got a charisma that makes everyone around her want to get up and do something fun," Tadhg told *Teen* magazine. "She can make even the longest scenes fly by with her upbeat personality and sense of humor."

Jordan Calloway. Jordan plays Addie's offbeat best guy friend, Zach. One minute he's standing up for causes he believes in (in one episode he goes to school barefoot to protest the underpaid workers who make sneakers), and the next he's shooting hoops for the school basketball team. Off the set, Jordan describes himself as a "sports nut" who's "hyper, talkative, and likes people for who they are, not what they are." He's also one of the ultimate pranksters on the *Unfabulous* set. "I'm always looking for ways to make people laugh," he told *Tiger Beat*. Before *Unfabulous*, you might have seen Jordan on *The George Lopez Show* or in commercials for Coca-Cola.

Malese Jow. Malese plays Addie's outrageous best girlfriend, Geena. She loves getting the school principal all riled up by wearing skirts that are several inches too short. But that's part of her charm—she's totally comfortable with who she is and doesn't care what anyone else thinks! Malese, who recently starred in the Disney Channel movie *Tiger Cruise*, was most excited to play Geena because of the unusual clothes she wears. "She is such a loud and funky dresser," she told *Tiger Beat* of Geena's crazy wardrobe. Off camera, Malese and Emma are just as close as they are on camera. "I think Emma's unique and confident personality makes her fabulous!" Malese revealed to *Teen* magazine.

Emma

Emma is always in style
on the red carpet

Here she is at the premieres of . . .

Superman Returns...

Pirates of the Caribbean 2...

© 2006 Getty Images

© 2006 Getty Images

The Ringer, with Haylie Duff and Arielle Kebbel, and . . .

The Family Stone.

Emma has a blast wherever she goes!

At the premiere of her own movie, *Aquamarine*, Emma and JoJo blew kisses to everyone . . .

and joined Sara Paxton in posing for the cameras.

Emma and Ludacris slapped hands with the crowd at the Nickelodeon Kids' Choice Awards in 2006.

© 2006 Getty Images

© 2004 Getty Images

Emma shares a joke with fans.

Emma loves her family!

© 2004 Getty Images

Emma and her mom, Kelly, at the *Grand Champion* premiere.

Emma with her dad, Eric, and stepmom, Eliza.

© 2004 Getty Images

Aunt Julia has been guiding her career.

It's fun hanging out with Aunt Julia's husband, Danny Moder.

© 2006 Getty Images

© 2004 Getty Images

© 2006 Getty Images

Simply Fabulous!

"Most of the time she is never like her character Addie Singer; she is very outgoing and energetic! There's never silence when Emma is around!"

Now that you've gotten to know the cast of *Unfabulous* a bit better, you can just imagine what a great and lively group they are to be around. And you can understand why life on the *Unfabulous* set never feels like hard work to Emma—it's way too much fun! "Despite the title *Unfabulous*, working on the show has been one of the most fabulous experiences of my life," Emma wrote on nick.com. "Most of the movies I have done haven't had a lot, or any, kids in them, so working on a show that is basically all kids has been so much fun. On breaks we hang out and play Xbox and foosball."

Even when Emma and her cast mates actually do work and film their scenes, they always end up laughing and making jokes. "We really try to have all our lines memorized," Emma told *Tiger Beat*. "But we mess up *all* the time!" The set of *Unfabulous* sounds like a never-ending party!

Emma never knows what kind of crazy situation Addie and her friends are going to find themselves in. That's part of the fun of being on the show. Addie's mishaps always make for interesting scenes to film! In the very first episode, Addie finds herself facedown in a big bowl of red fruit punch! Emma didn't quite know what she was about to get herself into when she agreed to stick her head in the punch bowl on the refreshment table. "I put my head in too hard and the table broke!" Emma admitted to *Teen People* magazine. "A bunch of guys came running over, trying to lift up the table and stay out of the shot. I'm in the punch bowl going, 'This is just great.'" But Emma loves playing Addie because getting into awkward situations is just one of many things they have in common! "Sometimes embarrassing things happen to me, too," Emma told *Today*. "When I was eight years old, I was jumping rope wearing over-sized army pants and they fell right off!"

The cast and crew of *Unfabulous* have also played tricks on Emma. One time she realized that a doll from the set, named Priscilla, was nowhere to be found. Priscilla was a doll in the hair and makeup department that all the girls used to experiment with new makeup looks and hairstyles. "Me and everyone else in hair and makeup made 'Have you seen her?' flyers partially as a joke, but weeks went by and still no sign of Priscilla!" Emma wrote on nick.com. "I was eating lunch one day when I found an envelope on my chair. It was a ransom note! I had to bring red gummy bears and an Oreo to the bathroom in the hair and makeup room!" Emma was convinced that Jordan had stolen Priscilla, but when she got to the bathroom, it turned out that *everyone* on the set was in on the joke! That was actually the start of an out-and-out war between the girls and the boys on the set of *Unfabulous*, which has taught Emma a lesson. "One day, me and Malese went into the boys' dressing room and we squirted shaving cream all over the place," Emma told *Sweet 16* magazine. "Then we went to open the door and our hands were so covered with cream that we couldn't turn the doorknob! We were stuck in their room and had to use the phone to call downstairs to have someone come get us out!"

With so many memorable moments on and off the set, Emma was sad when it was time to wrap filming on the first season. During their last week Emma wrote on nick.com, "I am happy and sad all at the same time. The people on the set become your family for three months and then we all have to leave!" The entire cast and crew of *Unfabulous* celebrated the end of a hugely successful first season of the show with a party at an arcade in Los Angeles called Jillian's. And besides, there wasn't anything to really be sad about. They would soon be back to start filming the second season of their show. And the show is now in its third season!

Here's a look at some of the highlights from the very first season of *Unfabulous*. Check out some of the humiliating things that Addie has to endure. It might make you blush just reading them!

The Party. When a back-to-school party is canceled because the host sprains his ankle, Addie steps in and offers to have the party at her place! But she doesn't realize that the popular girls are coming only because they love her big brother, Ben!

The Honesty Policy. Addie draws up a contract for her friends Zach and Geena to sign after she discovers they tell her little white lies all the time! But hearing the truth turns out to be a little more than Addie bargained for.

Picture Day. When one of the popular girls tells Addie that her hair looks "flat" on school picture day, she tries to fix it—but it just looks worse and worse! So Addie must decide if she is brave enough to take the picture with a horrible hairdo. If she doesn't go through with it, a haiku will replace her picture in the yearbook, and Addie's not sure which is more humiliating.

The Book Club. Even though Addie loves spending quality time with her mom, she cannot stand the mother-daughter book club they have joined. It's just way too boring and Addie doesn't know how to tell her mom without hurting her feelings, so she starts making up excuses to miss the meetings instead.

The Pal. Addie's crush is the adorable Jake Behari. And he just might like her back—until Geena puts in her two cents. She doesn't think Jake sees Addie as anything more than a friend! So Addie takes some desperate measures. She gets all dolled up, starts reading glossy teen magazines, and wears six-inch heels to get him to see her as more than a pal—but it doesn't work quite as planned.

The Pink Guitar. Addie feels ignored by her family and friends so she decides the best way to get their attention is to become famous. She joins an all-girl band called CUTE. It looks like CUTE could be the big break Addie needs—until she discovers the members of CUTE only *pretend* to play their instruments and sing songs!

The Rep. As a class experiment, Addie and her classmates are assigned to hang out with a specific clique for the entire week. Even though it's just a school project, Addie's stint as part of the "popular" crowd starts to change her for the worse. And it even begins to ruin her friendship with Geena—who is assigned to hang with the AV geeks.

The 66th Day. To celebrate sixty-six blissful days of liking Jake Behari, Addie makes a CD with sixty-five songs she has lovingly written about him! But all hell breaks loose when the CD somehow gets lost in the school! Addie goes on a desperate search to find it before it ends up in the wrong hands.

The List of the Kissed. In the girls' bathroom at

school, the popular girls keep a running list of those who have kissed a boy. Desperate to stop being ridiculed and finally make it onto the list, Addie goes on a hunt to find her perfect first kiss. But finding that special someone isn't quite as easy as Addie had hoped.

Chapter 7

Fashionista in Training

Whenever Emma is out and about—from a movie premiere to just hanging out with her friends—she always looks perfectly put together from head to toe. And with very good reason! Emma is a fashion maven. If it's in style, it's most likely hanging in Emma's closet—there is no doubt about that. When Emma isn't acting or keeping up with her homework, it's safe to assume she is shopping. Emma loves to keep up with the latest and greatest in the fashion world. She enjoys helping the wardrobe crew pick out Addie's clothes, and she loves coordinating outfits whether they are for her or for Addie. In fact, one day Emma may stop acting so she can pursue a career in fashion. Emma even said on nick.com that if she could have any other job in the world, she would be a fashion designer for Marc Jacobs. He is one of Emma's favorite designers; many of the most fashionable stars on the red carpet adore him as well! Emma's other favorite labels include Juicy Couture and Da-Nang. To sum up just how obsessed Emma is with fashion, all you have to do is meet her cat: Emma actually named him Coco Chanel!

Just as Emma has had acting on the brain since she was a little girl, fashion has always been on her mind too. "I was looking through old drawings and old stories I wrote when I was little, and it said I wanted to be a fashion designer," Emma told U.dailybulletin.com. "And I still do now want to be either a fashion designer or an actress. Both just seem like really interesting jobs and you can travel and just meet really cool people." Well, Emma really has the best of both worlds when you think about it. She's traveled all over the globe because of her acting career and hung out with some of the coolest (and most fashionable) people in the world. And fashion plays a very important part in every aspect of her acting career—from filming scenes to attending Hollywood events to traveling. Emma gets to wear stylish outfits to red-carpet events, and every time she films a TV show or movie, she gets an entire wardrobe of clothes her size to raid!

Emma is actually on her way to having a fashion career. She has modeled for Abercrombie and Fitch and appeared on the cover of hot fashion magazines like *ELLEgirl*, *Your Prom*, and *Teen*. She also just took over for Lindsay Lohan as the face of Dooney and Burke in their new advertising campaign. So what is next for Emma's modeling career? She secretly wants to take over for Mischa Barton as the face of Keds. "I want to be the Keds girl so bad," Emma told *Justine* magazine. "It's like my dream."

Emma's keen sense of style has even impressed

editors at major fashion publications. They've noticed how great and well put together Emma always looks, both on and off screen. Because of that, Emma's been invited in the past few years by the *New York Times* and *Women's Wear Daily* (the bible of the fashion industry) to model clothes and discuss her favorite things about fashion. That's very impressive for a sixteen-year-old girl. It's rare that someone so young ever gets taken seriously in the world of fashion.

Whenever Emma is on the set of *Unfabulous* she can't believe her good luck as she goes through racks and racks of clothing to put together outfits for Addie. "I think Addie's style is close to mine, so it's a lot of fun," Emma said on *Today*. Emma admits that she religiously reads every fashion magazine she can get her hands on. After all, she needs to make sure she doesn't miss a single new look or hot trend. Emma's biggest fear is that she'll make one fashion faux pas on the red carpet and end up on one of those "fashion victim" pages you see in the tabloids!

Emma also pays close attention to what her fellow members of young Hollywood are wearing in their movies and on the red carpet at Hollywood events. One of her fashion favorites these days is Ashley Olsen—more so than her sister Mary-Kate. "I like the way [Ashley] dresses," Emma told *USA Today*. "Mary-Kate's a little more thrown together, and Ashley is more elegant." Emma also loves the less revealing looks that Paris Hilton has sported. "Paris has cleaned up her look a lot," Emma added. "She's wearing nice suits now." Emma's all-time favorite movies are *Legally Blonde* and *Mean Girls* because of "the cute clothes," she told *U Daily Bulletin*. Who didn't love Reese Witherspoon's all-pink ensembles in *Legally Blonde* or Lindsay Lohan's trendy miniskirts matched with pink Ugg boots in *Mean Girls*?

Emma's personal style is very natural and always comfortable. Unless she's decked out for a red-carpet event, you'll never catch Emma in high heels or makeup. She doesn't wear makeup on a regular basis because her mom won't allow it. All in all, Emma's rule when it comes to fashion is to simply be herself. "I like to be casual and comfy," she told the *New York Times*.

The other thing Emma likes is a lot of one certain color adorning her wardrobe. "I'm like Elle Woods—I love pink," she told *Your Prom* magazine. Emma is also meticulous when putting together outfits. "I know what I like and I always want to find the perfect outfit for The Occasion," she added. "Sometimes it drives me crazy if I can't find exactly what I've pictured in my head." Emma usually doesn't have that problem because she has a keen personal style. "I like cute dresses and colorful, comfortable stuff like jeans or a jean skirt and a casual top," she describes to *Sweet 16*. "I love, love, love high heels." One thing Emma is very cautious of is dressing age appropriate. "You won't catch me in anything low cut . . . I'd feel naked!" she explains. "Don't you wonder about people who walk around wearing just a little piece of fabric? It's disgusting.

You have to figure girls in those skimpy outfits are insecure or maybe they're desperate for attention and want to shock people. It's not very cool." One of Emma's dreams is to design her own clothing line. "I hope to have my own line of clothing [one day]," Emma revealed to the *New York Times*. "I'd do one line of cute tops, pants, and bags and one line of evening gowns that people would wear to the Oscars!" It doesn't hurt that Emma's even had a little bit of experience with Oscar attire. When Julia Roberts won the Best Actress Oscar in 2001, Emma had the final say on what her aunt wore to the big event. After going through racks and racks of dresses from the most fabulous and famous designers in the world, Emma gave Aunt Julia the thumbs-up on a slim black-and-white 1982 Valentino gown. To this day, that dress is one of Julia's most recognized and famous looks. When she wore it, Julia looked like a princess, and no one will ever forget how beautiful she was—thanks to Emma!

Emma may love clothes, but purses are probably

her greatest weakness! "I've always loved to pick out my clothes … and I have an obsession with bags," she told the *New York Times*. She just can't resist adding a great bag to her enormous collection. "Whenever I get an allowance or any money, I always buy a purse," Emma confessed to *Teen People* magazine. "My mother will go, 'Emma, you have a thousand purses!' But I always need another—I'm obsessed with them!"

Emma would love it if her fans noticed her fashion sense and started looking to her as a trendsetter. Her fans always notice the cute clothes she wears on *Unfabulous* and talk about them on the Web! But Emma realizes that if she wants people to admire her sense of style, she needs to take better care of her clothes. Otherwise she may not have anything left to wear! She confessed to *Women's Wear Daily*, "My mom always says, 'If you don't clean up your clothes, I'm going to throw them away!'"

Chapter 8

Living the Surreal Life

As soon as *Unfabulous* became a bona fide hit for Nickelodeon, Emma was in high demand! In the blink of an eye, she was getting her hair and makeup done for magazine photo shoots and showing Maria Menounos from *Entertainment Tonight* around the set of *Unfabulous*. She got to appear on talk shows like *Live with Regis and Kelly*, *The Tony Danza Show*, *The Late Show with David Letterman*, and *The Ellen DeGeneres Show*. Visiting Ellen's show was a total blast! Ellen had heard that

Emma and her aunt Julia loved to knit together, so Ellen had a very special present to give to Emma. She gave Emma a very cute pair of sneakers that she had knitted herself! Emma put the shoes on immediately. She told Ellen, "These are going to be the new rage!"

The gift exchange didn't stop there. Emma brought a necklace with a shiny stone in the middle for Ellen. It matched the one Emma was wearing around her neck that day. Ellen loved it! But there was still one more surprise. Ellen gave Emma her very own Segway (a cool motor-powered scooter that you stand on), complete with a front plate that said "Emma." Ellen brought her own Segway out and they rode their Segways around the studio! It was a moment to remember! There's no denying it—Emma's life has changed and she's now a full-fledged star!

When Emma wasn't appearing on the likes of *Today*, she was making special appearances just for Nickelodeon. An exciting night for her was sitting in the audience of the Kids' Choice Awards presentations. But one of the craziest things Emma ever got to do was appear on the *On-Air Dare* segment. Every Saturday night on Nickelodeon, the cast of the sketch-comedy series *All That* challenges different Nickelodeon stars to participate in crazy (and sometimes gross) stunts during commercial breaks. Emma competed against *All That*'s Jack De Sena in an unusual race to shave the most hockey players' armpits! Disgusting, right? Totally! Emma was a real sport—and she won! But not everything Nickelodeon has asked Emma to do is always this gross. She got to play Addie in another Nickelodeon show! Emma appeared in an episode of *Drake & Josh* as a friend of Drake's sister, Megan. You know you've hit the big time when your character is so popular that she's recognized on other shows!

Emma's newfound fame gave her some wonderful opportunities to do some good for others too. During the 2004 holiday season, Emma was invited to a party at the home of renowned talk-show host Dr.

Phil for thirty children whose parents were military personnel based in Iraq. A host of other celebrities attended the event, including Kelsey Grammer, who read "'Twas the Night Before Christmas" to the children, *Desperate Housewives* star Marcia Cross, and former Nickelodeon actress Melissa Joan Hart. Christy Carlson Romano, famous for starring on the Disney Channel show *Even Stevens*, and the rapper Lil' Romeo performed during the party. Emma's job was to hand out presents to the children.

With all the extra attention that Emma was enjoying, there was one small downside. Suddenly the media and the tabloids were interested in more than her acting chops—they were interested in her personal life. It's not like Emma has anything to hide, but she does have famous relatives and that always makes for interesting tabloid fodder. Yet Emma handles the media's interest in her personal life in stride. "Of course not everybody is going to say good things about you. And yeah, you might be in the *National Enquirer*, but you know that what they report is not true so . . . and I'm a kid. I probably won't be on the cover of that anytime soon," she explained to U.dailybulletin.com. Plus Emma and Julia never let the fascination the media has with Julia's life affect their relationship. "It's not like I talk to my aunt about that," she told the *Alameda Times-Star*.

In fact, Emma has quite a hard time wrapping her head around the fact that people know her name and want to find out as much about her as possible. "I don't think of myself as a celebrity," Emma explained to *Your Prom*. "When people ask for pictures and autographs . . . that's still really weird for me." It's also weird when Emma hears things about herself in the press that are just simply not true. "I was on the set of *Unfabulous* when my co-star Malese came up to me and said, 'Oh my God, Emma, I didn't know that you and Emma Watson were having a fight!'" Emma told *Teen* magazine. "I look at the magazine and it said, 'The Emma Feud Is On' or something like that. I've never even met Emma Watson and I'm actually a fan! I love the Harry Potter movies. It's just like because both of our names are Emma we're in a fight!" It's definitely an annoying part of being on a hit TV show but Emma is learning little by little not to let it get to her.

Emma finds that friends can help her deal with all the increased attention. One friend in particular also has a famous relative. Jamie Lynn Spears, whose older sister is Britney Spears, also stars in her very own sitcom for Nickelodeon called *Zoey 101*. Jamie Lynn and Emma became fast friends and confidantes because they have a lot in common. Emma confronts constant questions from the press about Julia—they ask about everything from the twins to her relationship with Danny! It's tough for Emma because she loves her aunt and never wants to say anything that might be misconstrued or taken out of context. But trying to answer questions about Julia can be as difficult as what Jamie Lynn goes through. For years the tabloids have been obsessed with her sister, Britney, so they hound Jamie Lynn as a way of getting answers to all their questions. They ask Jamie Lynn about Britney's relationship with Justin Timberlake, her marriage to Kevin Federline, and her children. It's no wonder that Emma and Jamie Lynn were drawn to each other when they met at the premiere party for Nickelodeon's block of shows on TEENick. They had much to discuss! "Just like Jamie Lynn, when I see my aunt or my dad, we don't talk about the business or the press that they've gotten," Emma told *USA Today*.

The new friends discovered they had plenty more in common than exchanging tips on dodging the press. Emma and Jamie Lynn also loved hanging out and doing fun things together. "Emma's really cool," Jaime Lynn told *Entertainment Tonight*. "We went and saw a movie together. It was cool." The girls also got to pose together in *Teen People* for a spread in the "Young Hollywood" issue! It sounds like they're going to be friends for a long time to come. After all, it's important to have people to lean on who really understand what it's like growing up in Hollywood—and in the public eye!

A great new friend was just one perk of Emma's success. But as the newest "It" girl in Hollywood, all the movie studios were dying for Emma to star in their movies! Adding more movies to her resume is just fine with Emma . . . especially when she gets to be the leading lady!

Chapter 9

Leading the Way

In March of 2006, Emma made the biggest leap in her career. She landed the leading role in a major movie called *Aquamarine*. Her co-stars were pop singer JoJo (whom Emma was already an enormous fan of) and actress Sara Paxton, the star of the hit TV show *Darcy's Wild Life*. The movie is based on the popular novel by Alice Hoffman and it's about two teens (Emma and JoJo) who find a mermaid named Aquamarine in the pool at their beach club one summer (Sara plays the mermaid). Aquamarine falls in love with the cute boy who runs the food bar and begs the girls to help her set up a date with him.

Emma really loved the challenge of playing her character, Claire, because it was the most emotional and deep character she had ever taken on. One of the things that Claire experiences in the movie is the death of both of her parents. But playing such a wide range of emotions did pose some challenges. "It was difficult because on the set we all had a great time laughing so it was hard to get in the mode of sadness. I also just find it really embarrassing!" Emma told *Teen* magazine. "It's really hard, but it's something you just do and get it over with and when you're done you're like, 'Okay, let's move on.'"

But Emma really liked playing Claire. "She's so caring about everybody and wants to help. No matter how mean someone is to her, she'll always look at the bright side of that person or be positive in a situation that there is probably no positive outlook on," Emma added. "Claire is just really a great character that is really lovable."

Aquamarine was a magical experience all around, especially because Emma became best friends with JoJo and Sara. The three girls bonded while making the movie, especially since it was filmed in the far off—and beautiful—land of Brisbane, Australia, so they really had to stick together (and none of them minded!). When they weren't filming, the girls swam at the beach, rode their bikes, and ate a lot of pizza together. "I saved the crust for last and dipped it in ranch dressing," Emma revealed to *ELLEgirl* about their pizza parties.

The girls were also there for each other during some uncomfortable scenes to film. In the movie, Emma's character, Claire, is afraid of swimming with dolphins so she doesn't go through with it. "That was really hard for me to act that way because I love to swim!" Emma said to *Teen*. Ironically, JoJo's character does swim with the dolphins but it was JoJo who was petrified in real life! "I felt so bad for her—she was so afraid!" says Emma. Emma had such a wonderful time filming *Aquamarine* that she even helped herself to a souvenir from the set. "I took one of the signs from the Capri Beach Club that Claire's grandparents own," Emma told *Teen* proudly. "It's hanging up in my house."

Emma didn't think anything could top the experience of *Aquamarine*, but she was wrong. The next role she landed is the one that could very well turn her into a full-blown superstar. Emma will play Nancy Drew in the movie *Nancy Drew*. Emma is playing the famous character from the popular book series book that, chances are, your mom—and your grandma!—grew up reading! In the movie, "Nancy moves to L.A. from River Heights," Emma explained to *ELLEgirl*. "Her dad lets her pick their house, so she chooses one with a Hollywood mystery and unravels a murder." Emma is especially excited because the movie offers a first in Nancy Drew history. "The cool thing is that there's never been a murder mystery in any of the Nancy Drew books. It was always solving a mystery about something so this is the first one." The other cool thing about the movie is that even though it takes place in present day, Nancy still dresses like she is from the 1950s. "Nancy wears loafers, floods, and button-up shirts. I hate anything around my neck—I'm always pulling on the collar!" Emma confessed to *ELLEgirl* about her retro wardrobe. The funniest part of Nancy's offbeat ensembles is watching how others react. "She goes to Hollywood High and of course all of the kids there are in their trendy clothes and everything," Emma tells *Teen.*

Playing Nancy Drew was something Emma was absolutely dying to do. "I probably would have cried if I didn't get it," she told *Teen.* "Everyone knows who Nancy Drew is, except for my guy friends!" One of the most exciting parts about landing the role was when Emma found out that her dad was going to be played by actor Tate Donovan. Tate played Jimmy Cooper—Marissa's (Mischa Barton) dad on Emma's favorite show, *The O.C.* "I was so excited when I found out!" Emma said to *Teen*. "When I saw him for the first time, I said, 'I love *The O.C.*!'" From the day Emma landed the role, she has been doing her homework by reading Nancy Drew books. "I hadn't read them before, actually. I've started reading them now and I'm actually reading a book about the writer of Nancy Drew called *Girl Sleuth*," Emma told *Teen*. If all goes well at the box office, this could be the first of many Nancy Drew movies Emma will be making! Fingers crossed that we'll be seeing a lot more of her and those cute 1950s outfits at the box office!

After *Nancy Drew*, Emma is slated to start filming the teen comedy *Camp Couture*, where she plays a spoiled teen who's sent to a run-of-the-mill camp for the summer, instead of an elite fashion resort.

Something else in the cards for Emma is college, particularly New York University. "I love New York so much," Emma told *ELLEgirl*. "I want to study photography and I also love fashion design."

Emma knows she is lucky to have had so many

amazing opportunities. But she doesn't take one minute of it for granted. Emma really is a typical teenager. She might have an extraordinary life, but Emma is surrounded by tons of people who make sure she stays as grounded as possible. "If they have a stable life, I believe [acting] is absolutely fine, if it's not overdone," Emma's mom told the *New York Daily News*. Besides, Emma only wants to be an actress as long as it's fun. Because if it's not, what's the point? "If I don't want to do something, they won't make me do it," Emma explained to the *New York Daily News*.

It doesn't hurt that Emma has relatives in the business to turn to for advice and encouragement whenever she needs. But Emma's secret to staying grounded is that she does not take her success for granted. Starring in a hit TV show and jetting around the world to film movies might look easy, but it's a lot of hard work. And for every audition Emma nails, there are many more that she would rather forget about. As she explained to *Teen Vogue*,

"I've gone on maybe a hundred auditions where I've never even been called back. A well-known relative can get you in the door, but talent and hard work are what counts . . . although it was pretty cool when my aunt Julia introduced me to George Clooney." And that's why we love Emma so very much! With all the amazing experiences she's had and all the movies and TV shows she's starred in—she *still* gets starstruck! As long as Emma remains an everyday, normal, starstruck teen, it's pretty certain that she'll be in the spotlight for years to come!

Chapter 10

The Astrology Zone

The ancient art of astrology can give you insight into your personality traits (the good, the bad, and the ugly sides) and give you insight into your life events in the past, present, and future. The basic premise of astrology is this: Astrologers divide the calendar year into twelve parts. Each part represents a different astrological sign, beginning with Aries and ending with Pisces. The date you were born determines your sign. Astrologers believe the cosmic order of the heavens is reflected in everyone's unique life. They say that the Sun, Moon, and all the planets have a significant influence over you—including everything from your personality to your love life! Let's learn a little bit about what Emma's sign says about her—and then read on to discover your own astrological sign, and what it says about *you*!

Born on February 10, 1991, Emma's astrological sign is that of Aquarius. In typical Aquarius fashion, she's friendly, honest, loyal, charitable, original, inventive, independent, and intellectual. Emma lives up to those Aquarian qualities. After all, Emma is one of the friendliest young stars around. She is the closest of friends with all her *Unfabulous* cast mates, and she has made great new friends with her *Aquamarine* costar JoJo and fellow Nickelodeon star Jamie Lynn Spears. And of course we all know how loyal and dedicated Emma is to her family.

Like most Aquarians, Emma likes fighting for causes, dreaming of the future, having good companions, and most of all—having fun! An important Aquarian trait of hers is independence, so it's no wonder that Emma is such a great actress. Making movies sometimes means that you have to leave your friends and family behind for extended periods of time. But like a true, independent Aquarian, Emma has the maturity to handle it all without breaking a sweat!

Okay, now it's your turn! Look at the chart below to discover your personal sign. Then see if you agree with the personality traits associated with it!

Aries (March 21–April 19): You're bold, impatient, and a natural-born leader. Put all those traits together and you're someone who people find simply irresistible!

Taurus (April 20–May 20): You can be quite stubborn. But you have a grounded and steady way about you that lets people know they can count on you when they need you!

Gemini (May 21–June 21): You're smart and creative.

But because Gemini is symbolized by a set of twins, you often feel like you're pulled in two different directions and sometimes can't make a decision.

Cancer (June 22–July 22): You're known for being a bit of a homebody. Family is your top priority and you're deeply intuitive and full of emotion.

Leo (July 23–August 22): You love to be the center of attention! The more adored you are, the happier you become. You can also be stubborn when you don't get your way!

Virgo (August 23–September 22): You're a perfectionist who loves things to be as organized as possible. Helping others gives you great satisfaction.

Libra (September 23–October 22): More than anything else in the world, you love to be in love! When it comes to conflict of any kind you do whatever you can to avoid it.

Scorpio (October 23-November 21): You're deep, mysterious, and don't need words to figure out what others are thinking. You are an expert at reading body language. When others hurt you, watch out—it takes a long time for you to forgive!

Sagittarius (November 22-December 21): You are always searching for answers to the things you want to know about. You love to travel, and finding new things—from people to food—is your passion.

Capricorn (December 22-January 19): You're conservative and practical, yet ambitious and strong. You know what's most important to you but you're not one to go ahead and take big risks for anything!

Aquarius (January 20-February 18): You're a rebel among your friends (and you have a zillion of them), and you're always looking ahead to what's hot and what's not.

Pisces (February 19–March 20): You have a big heart and rely on your keen intuition at all times. You'd much rather follow your gut than go with facts and figures to solve problems. You love to sit and daydream and just go with the flow!

Chinese Astrology

You can also learn a lot about yourself using the Chinese version of astrology, which is based on the lunar calendar and a twelve-year cycle where each year is represented by a different animal. Because the lunar year follows the cycles of the moon, it usually begins between late January and mid-February of the Western calendar.

According to Chinese astrology your personality and ultimate destiny are guided by the characteristics of the animal that represents your birth year. Emma was born in February 1991, at the end of the Year of the Horse. People born in this year are known to be energetic, good with money, and very fond of travel. And not just travel by airplane. They also often roam from one project to the next. Hmm, isn't that exactly what Emma does? She moves from one movie or TV show or project, like recording a CD, to the next! Sounds like acting is the perfect career for Emma!

So what's your Chinese astrological sign? Check the chart below and learn a little bit about your sign. Maybe you're a Horse like Emma too!

1986—The Tiger
You're sensitive and caring.

1987—The Rabbit
You're popular and known for having lots of friends and family around.

1988—The Dragon
You're smart, charming, and lucky in love.

1989—The Snake
You're intuitive and savvy when it comes to business.

1990—The Horse

You're full of energy and great with money.

1991—The Ram

You're creative and enjoy spending time alone.

1992—The Monkey

You're a total party animal and love to have fun.

1993—The Rooster

You're resourceful and a quick thinker.

1994—The Dog

You're loyal and faithful.

1995—The Pig

You're generous, kind, and have great manners.

1996—The Rat

You're clever and witty.

1997—The Ox

You're a natural-born leader.

Chapter 11

Emma and Her Favorite Things

Here's a complete guide to everything Emma—
and what rocks her world!

Full name: Emma Rose Roberts
Nickname: Emzie, Em, Emmer
Birth date: February 10, 1991
Sign: Aquarius
Parents: Eric Roberts and Kelly Cunningham.
Stepmom Eliza Roberts. Stepdad Kelly Nickels.
Famous family: Aunts Julia Roberts and Lisa
Roberts Gillan

Siblings: Half sister Grace Nickels and stepsiblings Morgan and Keaton Simons

Eye color: Hazel

Hair: Dirty blond

Height: Five feet, two inches

Fave food: Pizza, pasta, and rice and chicken

Fave color: Pink

Fave school subject: English

Fave car: Hummer (but a pink one)

Fave hobby: Drawing

Fave sport: Volleyball

Fave music style: Hip-hop

Fave movies: *Mean Girls* and *Legally Blonde*

Fave scary movies: *The Others* and *The Shining*

Fave pet: Her cats, Coco Chanel and Pirate

Fave book: "*Bras and Broomsticks* is my favorite book ever," Emma told *Sweet 16*.

Fave place to hang out: The Arclight movie theater. You have to reserve your seats in advance and a concierge introduces each movie!

Fave off-the-set activity: Summer camp

Role model(s): Her mom, Kelly, and Reese Witherspoon

Fave actresses: Reese Witherspoon and Kirsten Dunst

Fave clothes: Uggs—in pink, of course!

Fave Halloween costume: A witch

Fave candy: Nerds

Fave TV shows: *Lost* and *America's Next Top Model.* "*America's Next Top Model* is actually very educational because it's taught me how to pose and stuff," she told *ELLEgirl*.

Fave handbag: "My hot-pink Louis Vuitton is my favorite," she said to *Your Prom*.

Fave video game: SSX Tricky. "It's a snowboarding game," she told *Sweet 16*. "I went to Sun Valley and snowboarded for real."

Fave ice cream: Chocolate ice cream from Cold Stone Creamery with Reese's and Butterfinger mix-ins.

Fave model: Gemma Ward. "I love her style. She's my favorite model ever," Emma told *Justine* magazine.

Fave reading material: "I know this sounds really

weird, but I buy so many magazines," she said to *Justine* magazine. "Every month I buy like 50 magazines. I just go to the magazine stand and I take one of everything. I go up to pay and the guy just looks at me."

Fave creative projects: "I'm really into scrap-booking, making collages, and knitting scarves," she told *Sweet 16*. "And, more than anything, I love photography, especially taking portraits of people."

Fave Julia Roberts movies: *America's Sweethearts* and *My Best Friend's Wedding*

Fave musicians: Usher, Jesse McCartney, Ashlee Simpson, Michelle Branch, JoJo, Eminem, John Mayer, and Jessica Simpson

Fave restaurant: The one inside the Chateau Marmont (a famous hotel in West Hollywood)

Fave store: Planet Blue in Malibu, California

Fave jewelry: "Dangly earrings" from Claire's and Planet Blue

Fave pastime: Cooking. "I make really good peanut-butter cookies," Emma told Ellen DeGeneres during an appearance on her show. "I mostly like to bake."

Dream Hollywood kiss: "Probably Orlando Bloom," she told *Teen People*. "I think he's really cute and he seems nice."

Here are the answers to some burning questions about Emma that we thought you might have!

Who would Emma exchange gifts with, if she had her pick of anyone in the world? Her crush, Matt Damon! And what would the gift be? "I would give him a certificate to go out to lunch—with me!" she told *Popstar!* magazine

What's the one thing Emma wants that she doesn't already have? "It would be an older sister," she told nick.com. "Because I don't like being the oldest!"

Who would Emma trade places with if she could? "Keira Knightley," she told *Popstar!* magazine.

"Because she got to be in *Pirates of the Caribbean*!"

What is Emma's most prized possession? "I've had my blanket since I was born," Emma told *Popstar!*. "It's just a big rag now. My mom always makes fun of me, but I always sleep with it!"

What kind of movies does Emma want to make? "I like doing any roles, really," she told the *Vancouver Sun*. "I like doing comedy more than anything, but I'd like to do a horror movie one day."

What's in Emma's purse? When Emma appeared on *The Ellen DeGeneres Show*, she shared the contents of her purse on the air. So what does Emma carry around with her? A little pouch with lip gloss, a book to read, a wallet, her cell phone, house keys, a compact, and a daily planner because "it makes me feel important," Emma told Ellen.

Does Emma have a boyfriend? "I mean, I have

crushes on celebrities but I've never had a boyfriend or anything. When it happens, it will happen," Emma told *Sweet 16*. "But I do have a lot of guy friends. Guys are so easygoing! If you say you can't get together with them, they say, 'Okay' and that's it. But girls can get so dramatic. 'Why? Where are you going? Are you hanging out with somebody else? Are you mad at me?' Guys just don't get all bent out of shape."

What is Emma's beauty regime? "I always put lotion on my face because my face gets really dry," Emma told *Justine* magazine. "And then I just put on mascara, some blush, light pink eye shadow and lip gloss."

Does Emma plan to go to college? "I want to go to college so I'll have lots of options in my future," she said to *Sweet 16*. "I'm planning on going to an East Coast college to major in photography. I love taking black and white portraits and

Photoshopping images. And maybe I'll minor in fashion."

What is Emma's best piece of advice? "Don't be in a hurry to grow up," she told *Sweet 16*. "You get to be an adult your whole life but you only get to be a kid once!"

Chapter 12

Lightning Round!

Think you *really* know Emma Roberts? Prove it with these true or false questions!

1. Emma has a cat named Old Navy.

                                       T F

2. Emma's first movie was *Blow* with Johnny Depp.   T F

3. Emma and Aunt Julia love to go bowling and yoga class together.   T F

4. Emma plays Geena on *Unfabulous*.   T F

5. Emma's dad, Eric, starred on the hit WB show *What I Like About You*.   T F

6. Emma was an extra in Aunt Julia's movie *Notting Hill*.   T F

7. Emma plays the guitar on *Unfabulous* and in real life.   T F

8. Emma's favorite actress is Reese Witherspoon.
     T F

9. Emma has a huge collection of shoes.
     T F

10. Emma has a sister named Grace.   T F

11. Emma filmed *Aquamarine* in Madrid, Spain.
     T F

12. Emma's dad in *Nancy Drew* is played by Tate Donovan, an actor who has appeared on her favorite show, *The O.C.*   T F

13. Emma's astrological sign is Aquarius.
     T F

14. Molly Hagan, who plays Emma's TV mom, once guest starred on the TV show *Friends*.
     T F

15. Emma's aunt Julia fell in love with her husband Danny Moder on the set of the movie *Grand Champion*.   T F

16. Emma's costar in her movie *Spymate* is a tiger.
                    T F

17. The first set that Emma ever visited was for the movie *Final Analysis* when she was only two weeks old.   T F

18. Emma's grandparents were famous dance teachers in Georgia.   T F

19. Emma's aunt Lisa is an actress who has had parts in a few of Julia Roberts's movies.
                    T F

20. Emma starred in the short film *BigLove* that debuted at the Cannes Film Festival.   T F

21. Emma loves to play softball.   T F

22. Emma wants to be a fashion designer one day.
                    T F

23. The first single off the *Unfabulous* soundtrack was Emma's favorite song, "I Wanna Be."
                    T F

24. Emma has become great friends with fellow Nickelodeon star Amanda Bynes.　　　T　F

25. Emma wants to go to college in Los Angeles.

　　　T　F

26. Emma received a pair of knitted sneakers from Ellen DeGeneres when she appeared on her talk show.　　　T　F

27. Emma was in *Teen People*'s "Young Hollywood" issue.　　　T　F

28. Emma always sleeps with a bunny she has had since she was a baby.　　　T　F

29. Emma's twin cousins are named Hazel Patricia and Phinnaeus Walter.　　　T　F

30. Emma is close friends with Goldie Hawn's daughter, Kate Hudson.　　　T　F

31. Emma's mom, Kelly, is not an actress and never has been.　　　T　F

32. It takes Emma two hours to get her hair and makeup done on the *Unfabulous* set.

　　　T　F

33. Emma's character Addie Singer on *Unfabulous*

has a huge crush on a popular and hot guy at her school named Jake Behari.   T F

34. Emma helped her aunt pick out a vintage Valentino gown to wear to the Oscars in 2001.

                                                         T F

35. Aunt Julia won a Best Actress Oscar for playing Vivian in the movie *Pretty Woman*.   T F

36. Emma fell in love with a Cabbage Patch Kids doll that became the inspiration for a movie that her Aunt Julia produced for The WB.

                                                          T F

37. Emma's mom is married to a former bass player for the rock band Mötley Crüe.   T F

38. Emma lip-synchs the songs her character Addie sings on *Unfabulous*.   T F

39. Emma loves to bake and one of her specialties is a great batch of peanut-butter cookies.

                                                        T F

40. A doll named Penelope was stolen from the makeup room on the set of *Unfabulous* as a practical joke on Emma.   T F

41. One of Emma's costars in her movie *Grand Champion* was Natalie Maines of the popular country trio the Dixie Chicks.   T   F

42. Emma is not allowed to see her first movie, *Blow,* in its entirety until she is at least eighteen years old.   T   F

43. Emma got to attend a holiday party for children whose parents are in the military at the home of talk-show host Oprah Winfrey.

                                                T   F

44. The biggest practical joker on the set of *Unfabulous* is Tadhg Kelly, who plays Addie's big brother, Ben.   T   F

45. Emma's favorite movies are *Freaky Friday* and *Sweet Home Alabama*.   T   F

Answer Key:

1. FALSE! Emma's cat is named after the legendary fashion designer Coco Chanel!

2. TRUE

3. FALSE! When Emma and Aunt Julia get

together, they love to cook and knit. "I mostly just make scarves," Emma confessed to Ellen DeGeneres on her show.

4. FALSE! Emma plays Addie Singer—Geena is the name of her best friend on the show.

5. FALSE! Emma's dad, Eric, was on the hit ABC sitcom *Less Than Perfect*.

6. FALSE! Emma was an extra in Julia's romantic comedy *America's Sweethearts*.

7. TRUE

8. TRUE

9. FALSE! Emma cannot resist buying a new purse whenever she gets her allowance, and she has an enormous collection of purses.

10. TRUE

11. FALSE! Emma and her costars headed Down Under—to Brisbane, Australia.

12. TRUE

13. TRUE

14. TRUE

15. TRUE

16. FALSE! Emma's very special costar in *Spymate* is a chimpanzee.

17. TRUE

18. FALSE! Emma's grandparents (on the Roberts side of her family) were famous acting teachers in Georgia.

19. TRUE

20. FALSE! Emma's short film *BigLove* debuted at the Sundance Film Festival, a celebration of the best in independent films held every January in Park City, Utah.

21. FALSE! Emma is an ace volleyball player.

22. TRUE

23. TRUE

24. FALSE! One of Emma's great new friends is fellow Nickelodeon star Jamie Lynn Spears from *Zoey 101*.

25. FALSE! Emma can't wait to head east to New York City to attend college!

26. TRUE

27. TRUE

28. FALSE. Emma goes to sleep each night with a raggedy old blanket that she's had since she was a baby.

29. TRUE

30. FALSE! Emma is actually good friends with Scout Willis, daughter of Bruce Willis and Demi Moore.

31. TRUE

32. FALSE! Emma only needs thirty minutes to get camera-ready and gorgeous for *Unfabulous*.

33. TRUE

34. TRUE

35. FALSE! Julia won a Best Actress Oscar for the title role in the movie *Erin Brockovich*.

36. FALSE! Emma fell in love with an American Girl doll during a visit to the New York store. That doll became the inspiration for a movie Julia Roberts produced for The WB.

37. FALSE! Emma's mom is married to Kelly Nickels, who played the bass for the rock band L.A. Guns.

38. FALSE! Emma sings every single song on *Unfabulous* herself.

39. TRUE

40. FALSE! The name of the stolen doll was Priscilla.

41. TRUE

42. TRUE

43. FALSE! Emma attended a holiday party for children in the military at the home of talk-show host Dr. Phil.

44. FALSE! Jordan Calloway, who plays Zach, is the prankster on the *Unfabulous* set.

45. FALSE! Emma's favorite movies are *Mean Girls,* with Lindsay Lohan, and *Legally Blonde,* with Reese Witherspoon.

Chapter 13

Finding Emma

$\mathcal{E}$njoy these handy resources to make sure you never miss a minute of what's going on with Emma on and off the screen!

Emma's Project Timeline

Here's your complete guide to keeping up with Emma's career—in the past, present, and future!

1. *Nancy Drew* (2007) . . . Nancy Drew
2. *Aquamarine* (2006) . . . Claire

3. *Unfabulous* (2004–07) TV Series . . . Addie Singer
4. *Spymate* (2003) . . . Amelia
5. *Grand Champion* (2002) . . . Sister
6. *Blow* (2001) . . . Young Kristina Jung
7. *BigLove* (2001) . . . Delilah

Websites to Check Out

Looking for an Emma fix when *Unfabulous* isn't on the air or there are no movies starring Emma at a theater near you? No problem! Just turn on your computer and you can get your share of Emma twenty-four hours a day! Whole communities of Emma fans have created some great websites devoted to bringing you the latest Emma news. You can even interact with other Emma fans who are just as into this fabulous star as you are!

Fabulous Emma
http://www.fabulous-emma.com

Your source for all things Emma
http://www.emma-roberts.net/

The Internet Movie Database
http://www.imdb.com/name/nm0731075/

Emma Roberts's TV.com listing
http://www.tv.com/emma-roberts/person/
84874/summary.html

Nickelodeon
Visit the network's site to read Emma's
weekly blog, meet the other *Unfabulous* cast
members, interact with fans, and a lot more.
http://www.nick.com

Starpulse
http://www.starpulse.com/Actresses/Roberts,_
Emma/

About the Author

Lauren Brown has been a pop culture fanatic from the day she started watching MTV as a little girl. She grew up in Miami, Florida, where her friends could always count on her to answer their burning entertainment questions! While attending the University of South Florida, Lauren began her career as an intern at *Rolling Stone* magazine. Immediately after graduating college in 1999, Lauren moved to New York City and began working for *CosmoGIRL!* magazine, where she served as entertainment editor. She has also worked at *US Weekly* and *Inside TV*, and is currently a producer at Sirius Satellite Radio. She is also the author of *Lindsay Lohan: The "It" Girl Next Door*. Throughout her career, Lauren has interviewed a wide range of popular celebrities, including Ashton Kutcher, Kirsten Dunst, Mary-Kate and Ashley Olsen, Jessica Simpson, Anne Hathaway, Chad Michael Murray, and Ashanti. She currently resides in Manhattan.